HANDMADE CARDS

CARDS

FOR FUN!

by Dana Meachen Rau

Content Adviser: Melanie Bauer, Manager, Consumer Education & Communication, Fiskars Brands Inc., Madison, Wisconsin

Reading Adviser: Frances J. Bonacci, Ed.D., Reading Specialist, Cambridge, Massachusetts

Compass Point Books ✦ Minneapolis, Minnesota

Compass Point Books
3109 West 50th Street, #115
Minneapolis, MN 55410

Visit Compass Point Books on the Internet at www.compasspointbooks.com
or e-mail your request to custserv@compasspointbooks.com

Photographs ©: Steve Gorton, Cards made by Gillian Chapman, front cover; Charlotte de la Bédoyère/Search Press, 5, 15, 16 (left), 21 (front), 32–33 (front); Keith Chapman, 6, 7 (left), 23, 24, 25, 26, 27, 29, 30, 31, 36 (all), 37 (all), 38–39, 40–41; Sarah Fabian-Baddiel/HIP/TopFoto, 7 (right); Rupert Horrox, 8, 9 (left), 10, 11, 14 (top & middle), 36, 37; Nicolette Neish/iStockphoto, 9 (right), 12 (middle), 13 (middle); Sean Locke/iStockphoto, 12 (top); Jon Le-Bon/iStockphoto, 12 (bottom); Rafa Irusta/iStockphoto, 13 (top), 14 (bottom); Ronald Bloom/iStockphoto, 13 (bottom); Loretta Hostettler/iStockphoto, 16–17; Gina Goforth/iStockphoto, 18–19; Glenda Powers/iStockphoto, 19 (left); John Archer/iStockphoto, 20–21; Jaimie D. Travis/iStockphoto, 22; Claire Dassy/BigStockPhoto, 28; Kristen Johansen/iStockphoto, 32–33 (back); Galina Barskaya/iStockphoto, 34; Anness Publishing, 35 (all); Hayley Easton/iStockphoto, 42 (left); Martin Anderle/iStockphoto, 42 (right); Valerie Crafter/iStockphoto, 43 (left); Tomasz Tulik/iStockphoto, 43 (right); Jaimie Duplass/iStockphoto, 44; Sally Scott/iStockphoto, 45 (top); Jonas Engström /iStockphoto, 45 (bottom); iStockphoto, 47.

Editors: Lionel Bender and Brenda Haugen
Designer: Bill SMITH STUDIO
Page Production: Ben White and Ashlee Schultz
Photo Researchers: Suzanne O'Farrell and Kim Richardson
Art Director: Jaime Martens
Creative Director: Keith Griffin
Editorial Director: Nick Healy
Managing Editor: Catherine Neitge
Handmade Cards for Fun! was produced for Compass Point Books by Bender Richardson White, UK

Library of Congress Cataloging-in-Publication Data
Rau, Dana Meachen, 1971-
  Handmade cards for fun! / by Dana Meachen Rau.
    p. cm. — (For fun)
  ISBN-13: 978-0-7565-3279-6 (library binding)
  ISBN-10: 0-7565-3279-5 (library binding)
1. Greeting cards—Juvenile literature. I. Title. II. Series.
  TT872.R38 2007
  745.594'1—dc22   2007004680

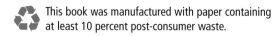 This book was manufactured with paper containing at least 10 percent post-consumer waste.

Table of Contents

Note: In this book, there are two kinds of vocabulary words. Card Making Words to Know are words specific to card making. They are defined on page 46. Other Words to Know are helpful words that aren't related only to cards. They are defined on page 47.

A Card for Every Event

On your birthday, you might eagerly run to your mailbox to see who has sent you a card. On a holiday, you might send cards to family and friends. Card stores have racks filled with cards for every occasion. There are cards for birthdays, weddings, and new babies. There are cards to send to someone who is sick. There are holiday cards for Thanksgiving, Valentine's Day, Christmas, Diwali, Id, and Hanukkah.

But you don't need to buy cards. You can easily make cards yourself. In fact, a handmade card is more than just a friendly greeting. By making a card, you are showing the receiver that he or she is worth the time it took you to create something special.

If you love to draw, you can create a beautiful picture. Even if you don't like to draw, you can create an image by layering different types of paper or making a collage of pictures. Your card can have a border and feature one item in the middle. Or it can have a pocket or a hidden flap. Just use your imagination!

Types of Cards

A basic card is a piece of paper folded in half, with the fold at the top or the left side.

A shape card is cut in a shape to reflect a theme.

A window card has an opening in the front so that you get a peek at the inside.

A pop-up card is a nice surprise. A picture on the inside jumps out when the card is opened.

Card Formats

Landscape format cards are wider than they are tall.

Portrait format cards are taller than they are wide.

Papyrus to Computers

More than 5,000 years ago, the ancient Egyptians shared good wishes for the New Year. They wrote notes to one another on slips of papyrus, a paper made from plants.

From the 1400s to the early 1800s, people exchanged cards for many occasions. But because they were handmade, they were expensive. Only wealthy people could afford to give them. In the mid 1800s, companies started printing cards to sell that did not cost as much. In 1840, when the world's first postage stamps began to be used, people could send cards farther and easier. Then commercial printing methods made it possible to create cards in factories. Many cards could

be made at once by a machine instead of each card being made by hand. Cards made by machines did not cost as much money. Hallmark and American Greetings, the two largest card companies today, had their starts in the early 1900s.

In the late 1900s, people began using computers to send cards. To send an e-card, you just have to go to a Web site, view the many types of cards available, and choose one to e-mail to a friend or family member.

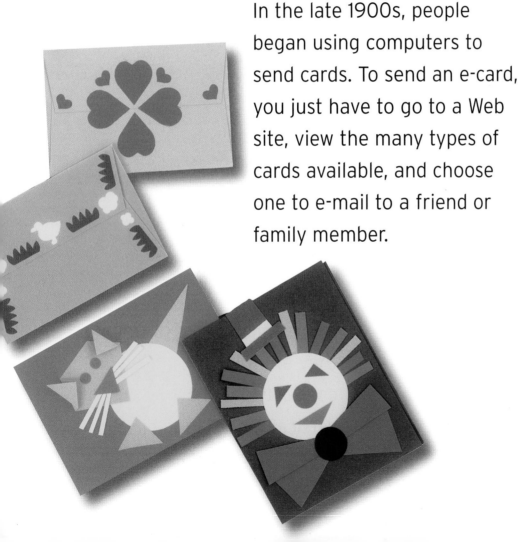

Valentine's Day

Valentine's Day is one of the oldest holidays associated with cards. In the Middle Ages, people sang love songs to one another. Handmade valentines have been found dating from 1415.

TO MY VALENTINE
Though a Golfing Match is most famous sport,
A much better match it would be
With hands united and true hearts plighted,
A love Match to make with me.

Ways to Fold

Whether you decide to create a basic card, a shape card, a window card, or a popup card, there are still choices to make while folding. Here are some ways to fold your cards.

When folding a card, it is important to measure accurately. With an easy-to-read ruler, measure from one edge in a few places. Using a pencil, mark where you want your fold. Connect the pencil marks with a line. Then fold the paper along the line, and push down along the crease with your finger to make it flat.

Single fold: Most cards are single-fold cards. This means they are folded in half. You can fold cards horizontally, vertically, or diagonally.

Gate fold: This type of card has two folds. The card is divided into three parts. The parts do not have to be equal. The sides fold in and overlap in the center.

Z and zigzag folds: These cards are divided into three or more parts. One end folds away from you, the next end folds toward you, and you repeat this as needed. From above, the paper is zigzag shaped.

Folding Paper

To make folds neat and creases flat, use a bone folder. A bone folder is a flat tool about the size of a pencil. Use it to score paper before you fold it by making a slight indent along the line where you are going to fold your card. Then you fold the paper away from you along this line.

Choices Galore!

In a craft store, you will see racks and stacks of paper. The paper comes in individual sheets and in big packs. Before you buy paper, though, check out what you might already have at home. These are some basic types of paper.

Card stock: This is a thick type of paper. Since you may want to layer more than one type of paper on a card, or glue on some three-dimensional details, you will need a thick paper like this as the base of your card. Poster board is thick, too, and can be used as the base for a card.

Vellum: You can see through vellum. It is sometimes patterned, but it often looks best over another decorative paper.

Decorative Paper

This paper is thinner than card stock and comes in many patterns. A sheet might be covered with flowers, stripes, bubbles, or leaves. You can often find the perfect paper to match the theme of your card.

Scraps

Stores sell bags filled with scraps of paper. Bags of scraps give you many choices when you are adding details to a card. But the best way to get scraps is to collect them yourself. Keep all scraps of wrapping paper, cardboard, tissue paper, or pictures from magazines.

Cut It Out!

Different shapes and different papers can make a card very exciting. So you'll need something to cut out those shapes!

Scissors: You'll need a pair of regular scissors to cut shapes from your paper. To cut out very small shapes, you can use nail scissors.

Tearing: You can tear paper to give it a rough edge. Or to get the edge nice and straight, tear the paper against the side of a ruler.

Paper edgers: These are scissors that make patterns as they cut. They come in zigzags, waves, and other shapes.

Craft knife: A craft knife is a very sharp tool that cuts straight lines in paper. Only use a craft knife with an adult's help. You will need a cutting mat or piece of cardboard under the paper you are cutting.

Punches: You may have seen a hole puncher that makes little circles. Punchers also come in star shapes, heart shapes, and more. Some punches cut out fancy borders or corners. Punches create two images. The shape you punch out is the positive image. The piece of paper with the hole in it is called the negative image. One way to create a starry night sky is to punch a piece of dark blue paper with a star punch and place a yellow piece of paper behind it.

Stick to It!

You have the paper. You've cut out your shapes. How will they all stick together?

Glue: For most projects, you can use white glue to layer papers and add details. However, don't squeeze on too much. Wet glue can make paper look bumpy when it dries. To glue papers together, you can use a glue stick. It gives you a little more control to make a thinner layer.

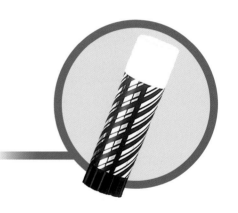

Tape: Double-sided tape is sticky on both sides. It is strong enough to hold layers of paper together. Some double-sided tapes are made of foam. The foam raises the paper up a bit so that it looks three-dimensional.

Sewing: Sewing holds fabric together, so why not try it with paper, too? Poke holes through two pieces of paper. Then thread one paper to the other.

Attaching Vellum

Since you can see through vellum, you can also see the tape or glue you use to stick it to other papers. Attach vellum by using a special see-through adhesive you can buy in a craft store.

Sticking Tips

When you glue or tape one paper to another, turn the paper wrong-side up. Spread glue over the paper, or put down your tape, especially on the corners and edges. Turn the paper over, and place it carefully where you want it, making sure it is straight. Rub over the paper to flatten it. Or place the card under a heavy book while it dries.

Write On!

If you are drawing a picture on your card, what will you use? Poster paint or watercolor paint can help you create beautiful pictures and details. You can also use crayons, colored pencils, or markers. Some markers are like paintbrushes with pointed but flexible tips.

Calligraphy

Calligraphy is the art of writing. Each letter is carefully crafted with a flat-edged pen that creates smooth strokes and details. Before the printing press was developed in the 15th century, all written material was done by hand. One of the jobs of religious men called monks was to copy important works in a decorative style. Even though we can use computers today to create all types of fancy writing, calligraphy is still a respected type of art.

Usually pens and markers don't show up well if you are drawing on dark-colored paper. You might want to use gel pens or paint pens. They show up very well, especially on dark blue and black paper.

Cards do not just have pictures. They need words, too. You can use any tools used to draw your pictures to also write the messages on the front and inside of your card.

Decorate!

If you don't like to draw, you can make pictures with stencils and stamps. A stencil is a cutout image. You trace around the edges of the stencil with a pencil to transfer the image to your card. To make an image with a stamp, you dip it in ink or paint, or color it with marker, and then press it onto your card.

Rubber stamps come in thousands of styles, and ink pads come in many colors. After you stamp, you can color in the image with pencils or markers. You can also make stamps out of sponges, potatoes, and carrots cut into any shape or design you want.

You can glue on decorations, too, such as small bits of paper cut into shapes or bits of fabric, lace, or ribbons. If your card does not have to go in an envelope, you can make the details really three-dimensional with buttons or beads.

Stickers don't even need glue. You can buy stickers of animals, carnival food, princesses, flowers, and many other objects.

Glitter Tips

Glitter can be a messy addition to a card, but it brings pizzazz to your creation! Here's what to do to keep your work neat:

1. With white glue, "draw" along the line or area where you want to add glitter. Keep the glue layer as thin as possible.

2. Sprinkle a lot of glitter on the gluey area.

3. Shake the extra glitter onto another piece of paper.

4. Bend the paper in half, and use it to pour the extra glitter back into the container to use again.

Planning First

Here are some card-making basics for each project you will do.

Think of Your Theme: Think about what type of card is best for the occasion. For example, you might want to make an upright zigzag card if you plan to draw something tall, such as a giraffe. For a card for a sports fan, maybe look for a decorative paper covered with baseballs or tennis racquets.

Sketch It Out: Don't start drawing or gluing items onto your card right away. First plan it out on a scrap of paper. If you are making more than one card, transfers and templates make the job easier.

Decide the Size: What size should your card be? If you need the card to fit in an envelope, measure your envelope first. Your folded card should be about $1/4$ inch (0.64 cm) smaller on all sides. If your card doesn't need to fit in an envelope, you can make the card any size you wish!

Copying Pictures

Transfer: Draw your image on tracing paper with a pencil. Flip it over, and draw over all your pencil lines. Flip the tracing paper back over onto the card. Redraw over your original lines. Your image will be transferred to the card.

Template: If you are going to cut your card into a shape, make the shape first with a piece of cardboard. Place the shape on your card, and trace along the edge.

Fancy Valentine

Valentines are some of the oldest cards in history. This heart-shaped card does not open. All the words and decorations are on the front. The fancier the card, the better!

1. Use sheets of pink glitter card and red card stock $8^1/_2$ by 11 inches (21.6 by 28 cm). Fold the pink card in half. Draw half of a heart shape with a pencil, with the center of the heart along the fold. With the card still folded, use scissors to cut out the heart. Make sure to cut through both layers of card.

2. Fold the red card in half. Using your pink heart as a guide, draw and cut a larger heart from the red card. From scraps of red card, cut two small hearts.

3. Unfold both the pink and red hearts, and lay them flat. Glue the pink heart into the center of the red heart.

4. With a hole punch, punch an even number of holes around the edge of the red heart. Starting at the

center top, thread the ribbon (about 45 inches/ 115 cm long) in and out of the holes. Tie the two ends of the ribbon in a bow. Attach the red hearts to a shorter ribbon and tie to the card.

5. Take the dots you punched out of the red heart, and glue them around the pink heart as a border.

6. Using letter stickers, or with a marker, paint pen, or gel pen, write your message in the center of the pink heart. Add heart stickers wherever they fit!

Materials

- 1 sheet of red cardstock
- 1 sheet of pink glitter card
- Pencil · Scissors · Glue
- Hole punch
- Ribbon
- Heart and letter stickers
- Marker, paint pen, or gel pen

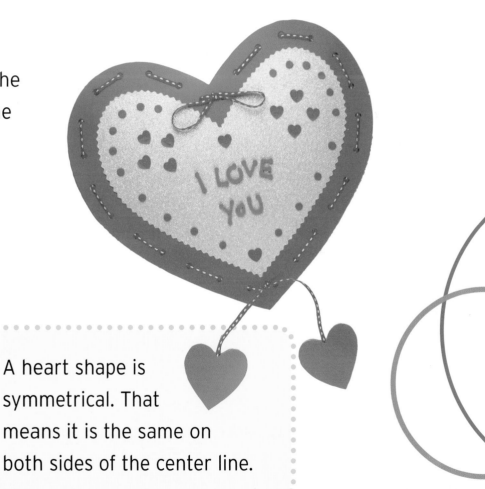

A heart shape is symmetrical. That means it is the same on both sides of the center line.

Party Invitation

This invitation is a window card. You can see inside the card even when it is folded shut. Here we have a house, where we get a peek at a party.

1. Use a sheet of card stock 8½ by 11 inches (21.6 by 28 cm). Fold the card in half. On the front of the card, glue a house shape, with two square windows and a rectangular door.

2. Unfold the card. Place a piece of cardboard or a cutting mat under the card. With a craft knife, cut out the square windows. Cut the door only on three sides, leaving one of the long sides uncut. Fold the door along the uncut side so it can open.

3. Finish decorating your house with markers, and glue on more details.

4. Use scissors to cut out balloon shapes of mixed sizes from scraps of other colored card stock.

5. Attach lengths of ribbon to some of the large balloon shapes. Glue one balloon and ribbon to the front of the card, and glue the rest inside the card on the right side. Glue smaller balloons without ribbons on the left side.

6. Write your message and invitation details on the balloons. You can use sticker letters on the front of the card, and write the details with marker, paint pens, or gel pens.

Materials

- 1 sheet of card stock
- Cardboard or cutting mat
- Craft knife
- Scraps of card stock of various colors
- Scraps of ribbon
- Scissors • Glue
- Markers, paint pens, or gel pens
- Sticker letters

Birthday Popup!

A simple pop-up card can give someone an added surprise. Be sure your measurements and folds are perfect, or your card might not pop-up or open properly.

1. Use two sheets of card stock 8½ by 11 inches (21.6 by 28 cm), one for the inside of the card and one for the outside. Fold the inside card stock in half. Find the center of the fold. Measure about 2 inches (5 cm) from each side of the center, and mark those points. Draw two evenly spaced lines about 2 inches (5 cm) long. Cut along these lines through both layers of paper with a scissors.

Materials

- 2 sheets of brightly colored card stock
- Sheet of white printer paper
- Scraps of other colored paper
- Scissors and ruler
- Glue stick
- Sequins, braids, stickers

2. Open the card. Fold the center area that you just cut toward you. Close the card again, rubbing firmly to be sure all the folds are flat.

3. Cut a rectangle of colored paper about 3 by 4$\frac{1}{2}$ inches (7.6 by 11.5 cm). Round off the top corners with the scissors. Decorate the rectangle like a fancy birthday cake, using sequins and braids. Open your card. Glue your cake to the front of the box shaped pop-up. Close your pop-up card and press it flat. This is now your inner card.

4. For the outside of the card, fold the second piece of card stock in half. Rub glue on the inner card, both front and back (but not on the back of the pop-up). Slip it into the outer card. Press the inner and outer cards together firmly.

5. Print your message onto a sheet of white paper. Cut around the message to make a speech bubble. Stick the bubble on the front of the card. Decorate the inside and outside of the card with lots of stickers.

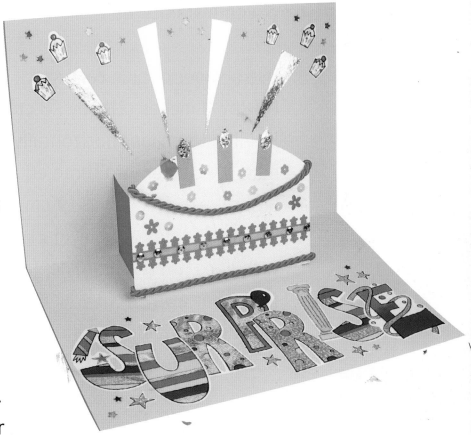

Snowman Card

You can create a winter greeting card with a stamp you make yourself!

1. Use a sheet of blue card stock $8^1/_2$ by 11 inches (21.6 by 28 cm). Holding the paper horizontally, mark the paper into three equal areas, each $3^1/_2$ inches (9 cm) wide, and connect your marks with lines. On the first line, fold the paper away from you. On the second line, fold it toward you. You now have a Z fold.

2. With scissors, cut out a circle from a sponge. (Wetting the sponge with a little water will help make it soft enough to cut.) This will be the stamp for your snowman.

3. Squeeze white paint onto a paper plate. Dip your snowman stamp in white paint. Blot off any extra paint onto a paper towel. Stamp three circles on the last third of your card for your snowman. Stamp the bottom quarter of the whole card to make snow on the ground.

4. Dip the handle end of a paintbrush into the paint. On the top three quarters of the card, dot the paint in the sky to make falling snow.

5. While the snowflake paint is still a little wet, sprinkle on glitter. Shake off the excess. (See glitter tips on page 19.)

6. When the paint is dry, add details to the snowman with markers. Use letter stickers to write a message on the snow. Glue on scraps of colored card stock to make a scarf and hat.

Materials

- 1 sheet of blue card stock
- Ruler and pencil
- Scissors
- Sponge
- Paper plate
- White paint
- Paintbrush
- Glitter
- Stickers
- Glue
- Scraps of colored card stock
- Markers

Nature in an Envelope

People often enjoy cards made from natural materials. You can add messages to these cards, if you wish. Or they could be for letters you write to friends.

1. Use a sheet of card stock 8$\frac{1}{2}$ by 11 inches (21.6 by 28 cm) or a little smaller. Fold the sheet in half. This will be your base card.

2. By hand, tear a scrap of light-colored paper to make a rectangular piece about 4 by 6 inches (10 by 15 cm).

3. Place the light-colored paper over leaves. With an unwrapped crayon held lengthwise, rub over the paper. You will leave impressions of the leaves on the paper.

4. Put glue or double-sided tape on the back of the paper. Place it in the center of the front of your card.

5. Glue bits of pinecone or other seeds around the rubbing to make natural borders. You can also glue dried leaves directly onto the paper scrap.

Making a Statement!

Sometimes the words to put in a card are easy to think up. "Happy Birthday!" "Get Well Soon!" "I Love You!" "Happy New Year!"

You can borrow words from someone else to express how you feel. Cards can include famous quotes or words from songs or poems. You can use a quote by your favorite character in a book, play, or movie.

Your card can make people laugh if you include a joke. For an "I Miss You" card, you could say: "Why did the chicken cross the road? Because he missed you!"

Joke Ideas

For a Halloween card, you could draw a spooky ghost with these words: "What did the ghost say when he stubbed his toe? Boo hoo!"

Pun Ideas

A pun is another kind of joke. A pun is when you replace one word with another word that sounds the same but has a different meaning. For example, if you drew a bumblebee on your valentine, you could write "Bee Mine."

Rhyme Ideas

You can write a simple poem. You just need to find a few words that rhyme. How about this for a birthday card:
"It's your birthday. Have some cake! I think you are really great!"

In Any Style

The world is filled with beautiful styles of art. You can use some of these styles in cards you make.

Indonesian Batik

Batik is an art in which cloth is treated with wax in certain areas and then dipped in dye. The wax areas stay white while the rest of the cloth soaks in the color. On a card, you can draw a design, pattern, or picture with white crayon on white paper. Then paint over the whole card with watercolor paint. Your crayon lines will stay white.

Happy Birthday Around the World

Greeting cards around the world may look similar, but the language is different. An American card might say "Happy Birthday," but in Mexico it might read "Felíz Compleaños," in France "Joyeux Anniversaire," and in Japan "Otanjou-bi Omedetou Gozaimasu."

Greek Mosaic

The ancient Greeks and Romans made pictures out of small glass tiles. Through history, this mosaic art spread to many cultures of the world. To create a mosaic on your card, you can use bits of paper instead of glass.

German Woodcutting

Germans have a 600-year tradition of printing designs in Christmas cards with woodcuts. With adult help and special woodcutting tools, you can cut a design or picture into a block of soft wood, cover it with paint, and stamp it onto a card, like a rubber stamp. You can use blocks of potato, sponge, foam, and plastic instead of soft wood to make your designs.

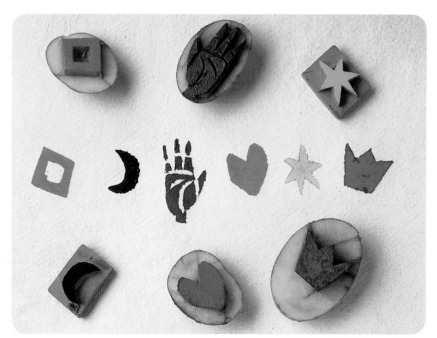

Celebrate With Cards!

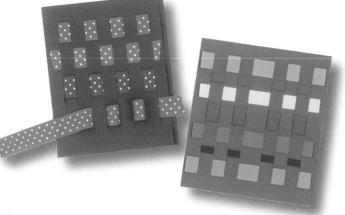

Many holidays we celebrate today have long histories. New Year celebrations have existed since the beginning of recorded time. Seasons, birthdays, and anniversaries have long been marked with special celebrations. Cards have become an important part of many events.

Make nice designs on the front of your cards, and write your messages inside.

Snowmen and pine trees are popular designs for Christmas cards.

Cards offer a way to send good wishes to someone you may not see, or even to those you see every day.

Christmas is the most popular card-giving holiday. Stores sell cards in big boxes, and the post office has to handle thousands of extra pieces of mail.

Valentine's Day is the next most popular card-giving holiday. Children at school often exchange cards with everyone in their classes. Sometimes they make special Valentine's Day mailboxes to hold all their cards!

Some holidays do not have a long past. Popular card-giving holidays, such as Mother's Day and Father's Day, have only been holidays for less than 100 years.

Designs make cards unique and beautiful.

Designing on the Computer

Some people use another tool to make cards or the messages to stick on them—the computer!

Many computers have programs that help you design cards. First you choose the type of card you want—basic fold, gate fold, postcard, and others. You can decorate your card with all types of borders, lines, and little pictures called clip art. If you have a digital camera, you can take photos, save them on your computer, and use them in your card, too. Then all you have to do is print out your creation.

RY SOON..!

Happy Birthday

Party Time

The words on your computer-created card can be as artistic as the pictures you choose. Computers have almost 100 types of fonts—styles of letters, numbers, and other symbols—to choose from. Some are plain. Some are fancy. Some may even look scary or silly. You can make your words any size you wish. You just have to decide which font best fits the occasion.

GOOD LUCK

Serif and Sans Serif

Most fonts are divided into two types, serif and sans serif. Serif means that most of the letters have little "tags" on the end of each straight line. Sans serif fonts do not.

Gillian Chapman Creative Crafter

Cards, scrapbooks, decorative boxes, jewelry, masks, and puppets—these are just some of the handmade crafts Gillian Chapman designs and creates. She is a champion craftsperson. Many of her handmade cards are featured in books and magazines around the world.

As a child, Chapman was always sketching, drawing, and making things by hand. Her family gave her the time to draw and use her imagination. At home, they set up a workshop where she could cut, paste, and sew. In high school, she couldn't stop doodling and designing. She spent many of her vacations creating gifts and decorative objects.

Gillian Chapman helps children create cards for all occasions.

After high school, Chapman continued her art studies at college. She learned and practiced design, illustration, and handicraft techniques. She then spent 10 years working with teachers in schools, giving workshops on all kinds of crafts. From this experience, she refined her skills of designing, writing clear and simple step-by-step instructions, photographing the creative process, and presenting the finished items. She was commissioned to write and produce many books on handmade crafts.

Chapman continues to work closely with children, inspiring and helping them create handmade cards and other items. She is inspired by everyday life and objects.

What Happened When?

| 3000 B.C. | 100 A.D. | 1300 | 1400 | 1500 | 1600 | 1700 |

3000 B.C.
Ancient Egyptians share good wishes on slips of papyrus.

100 Scissors made of two crossed blades (like the type we use today) are invented in ancient Rome.

1390 A mill that uses water power from a nearby river opens in Germany to make paper.

1415 The first handmade Valentine's card is made.

105 A court official in China invents a paper-making technique that uses rags left over from the making of textiles.

1452-1455 Johannes Gutenberg prints the first book mass published on a movable type printing press.

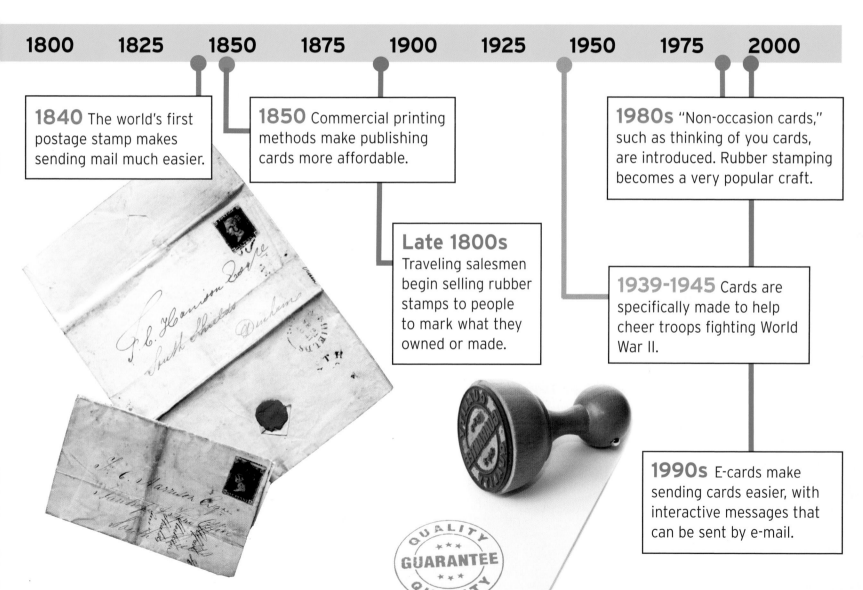

1800　　**1825**　　**1850**　　**1875**　　**1900**　　**1925**　　**1950**　　**1975**　　**2000**

1840 The world's first postage stamp makes sending mail much easier.

1850 Commercial printing methods make publishing cards more affordable.

Late 1800s Traveling salesmen begin selling rubber stamps to people to mark what they owned or made.

1980s "Non-occasion cards," such as thinking of you cards, are introduced. Rubber stamping becomes a very popular craft.

1939-1945 Cards are specifically made to help cheer troops fighting World War II.

1990s E-cards make sending cards easier, with interactive messages that can be sent by e-mail.

QUALITY ★★★ GUARANTEE ★★★ QUALITY

Fun Card Facts

In 1843, Sir Henry Cole of England hired an artist to design a card to have printed to send to his family and friends at Christmas. His cards are known as the first published Christmas cards, and he started the tradition of sending many cards to friends for the holidays.

Joyce C. Hall, the founder of the card company Hallmark, started selling his cards in 1910 when he was only 18 years old. He carried his postcards in a shoebox to show buyers.

Father's Day was founded by Sonora Dodd in 1910. She was grateful for the hard work of her father, who raised six children on his own after their mother died. It became a national holiday in 1924.

Not including holiday cards, the most popular cards are birthday cards. Next come anniversary cards, followed by get well cards, friendship cards, and sympathy cards.

Besides the many hole punches, scissors, and other materials you can buy at craft stores, you can also get tapes and ribbons of many colors and designs. You can use these to embellish your handmade cards.

45

Card Making Words to Know

basic card: piece of paper folded in half, with the fold at the top or left side

bone folder: card-making tool that helps you score the paper and flatten creases

border: decoration along an edge

calligraphy: art of writing

card stock: thick type of paper

collage: to bring together different images or objects to make a picture

craft knife: very sharp tool for cutting paper

crease: folded area

cutting mat: mat that protects your work surface from the craft knife

decorative paper: paper with designs already printed on it

die cutter: larger punch that cuts out shapes from paper

double-sided tape: tape that is sticky on both sides

edgers: scissors that cut decorative lines

fonts: different styles of letters, numbers, and other symbols

gate fold: card with two sides folding into the center

gel pens: pens that can write on dark paper

glitter: small bits of sparkly metal

impression: image left behind by rubbing

ink pad: spongy square of color that you use with stamps

paint pens: pens that can write on dark paper

pop-up card: a card with a picture on the inside that jumps up when the card is opened

poster paint: paint that is easy to use and cleans up with water

punches: tools that punch out shapes from paper

rubbing: using crayons to leave the impression of something on paper

score: to make an indent along the line you wish to fold

shape card: card cut into a shape to reflect a theme

single fold: card with one fold

stamps: cutout images that you put into paint or ink and press onto your card

stencils: cutout images that you can trace inside

template: cutout image that you can use over and over again to make more than one card

vellum: paper you can see through

watercolor paint: thin paint that cleans up with water

window card: card with a cutout in the front that shows a bit of the inside

Z fold: card with two folds, one toward you, and one away

zigzag fold: card similar to a Z fold but with more than two folds

Other Words to Know

batik: art form that uses wax and dye on fabric

commercial: for many people; made in a factory

commissioned: paid to perform a service

flexible: able to bend

mosaic: art form that uses small glass tiles to make a picture

negative image: space left behind when you cut out an image

papyrus: type of paper made from a plant

positive image: image you cut out

printing press: first machine that could put words onto paper; before it, people had to write everything by hand

sans serif: font in which the letters do not have tags on the end of each straight line

serif: font in which the letters have little tags on the end of each straight line

symmetrical: same on both sides of a center line

transfer: move from one place to another

woodcutting: art form that uses wood as stamps

Where To Learn More

AT THE LIBRARY

Cusick, Dawn, and Meg Kirby (eds.). *The Michael's Book of Paper Crafts*. New York: Lark Books, 2005.

Hufford, Deborah. *Greeting Card Making*. Mankato, Minn.: Capstone Press, 2006.

Winters, Eleanor. *Calligraphy for Kids*. New York: Sterling Publishing Company, 2004.

ON THE ROAD

Crane Museum of Papermaking
30 South St.
Dalton, MA 01226
413/684-6481

Robert C. Williams Paper Museum
Institute of Paper Science and Technology
Georgia Institute of Technology
500 10th St. N.W.
Atlanta, GA 30332-0620
404/894-5726

ON THE WEB

For more information on this topic, use FactHound.

1. Go to *www.facthound.com*
2. Type in this book ID: 0756532795
3. Click on the *Fetch It* button.

FactHound will find the best Web sites for you.

INDEX

ABOUT THE AUTHOR

Dana Meachen Rau has written more than 200 books for children, both fiction and nonfiction. She almost never buys cards at the store but instead has a drawer full of scraps of paper, fabric, buttons, and many of the items described in this book. When a holiday comes, she dives in and sees where her imagination takes her. She lives in Burlington, Connecticut, with her husband and children.